IN THE DRINK!

The sea isn't just a lot of blue, salty water. It's home for all sorts of living things...

And it's not always blue!
Sea water is often green because
there are billions of tiny green
plants living in it.

But to know what really goes on in the water,
you have to look beneath the surface...
Take a dip in the sea and **find out...**

how to help wildlife!

why the sea is salty!

how to find ancient coins!

what whales sing about!

Most people like to go **TO THE BEACH**

That's why it gets so crowded!
You have to keep your eyes open to spot
strange and interesting creatures...

WELCOME TO QUIZ BEACH!

*How many three-legged people
can you see in this picture!?*

£5.95

Class No. J551.46   Acc No. C/31332
Author: YARDLEY, T   Loc: 5 MAR 1996

LEABHARLANN
CHONDAE AN CHABHAIN

1. This book may be kept three ~~weeks~~.
   It is to be ret~~urned on or before~~ the last date
   stamp~~ed below~~.

J551.46/C31332

2. A fine ~~will be charged for~~ every week
   or part ~~of a week~~

9 NOV 1996		
2 2 NOV 1996		
	Cavan County Library	
	Withdrawn Stock	

ALL AT SEA!

The best way to read this book is to begin at the beginning and read all the way through.

You'll be amazed at what you'll find out.

But if you want to read about one particular thing, such as icebergs or plankton, look in the index on page 33.

Thompson Yardley wrote this book and drew the pictures. He has done a lot of other things as well as writing books, such as driving a dustbin lorry and looking after pigeons.

ISBN 0 304 32318 7

First published in 1990 by
Cassell Publishers Limited
Villiers House, 41/47 Strand
London WC2N 5JE

© Copyright Lazy Summer Books Limited

Printed and bound in Great Britain
by Eagle Colourbooks Ltd, Glasgow

There are lots of ways to play with **SAND**

You probably know how to make
sandcastles with a bucket and spade.
BUT... why not go for something more adventurous?..

HOW TO MAKE SAND SCULPTURES

1. Find an uncrowded bit of beach. Make a big heap of damp sand.

2. Use your hands to mould it into the shape you want.

3. Try using sea shells for eyes and seaweed for hair.

4. Add other items which you may find on the beach.

5. Stand back and watch people admire your work!

NEPTUNE ~
(GOD OF THE SEA)

CLIFF HANGERS

Sandy beaches often form where rocks and cliffs are worn down by the sea. Sometimes the base of the cliff is eaten away – leaving a dangerous overhang that you can't see. This bit could break off at any time!

Sea birds often make nests on cliffs and rocks. If you frighten them, they may leave their eggs unprotected.

Cliffs provide homes for all sorts of plants and animals. Cliff plants have strong roots to grip onto the rocks. But... they may not be strong enough to support your weight!..

Tell someone where you're going before you set off!

If you go exploring, watch out for falling rocks! AND... keep an eye on the sea. The tide may come in and trap you. You may be lucky and be rescued. Or perhaps you won't!

4

SHELL SHELTERS

200 million-year-old fossil shell

As the sea wears away cliffs, it washes out old rocks. Some of these are fossils – the stony remains of ancient animals.

Some of them look like present-day shells. Shells are the self-made homes of living creatures called molluscs. They collect limestone for their shells from rocks which have dissolved in the sea.

Modern mussel shell

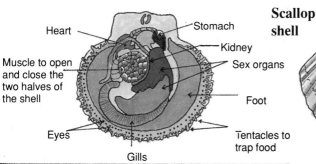

Heart
Stomach
Kidney
Muscle to open and close the two halves of the shell
Sex organs
Foot
Eyes
Tentacles to trap food
Gills

Scallop shell

1 year
2 years
3 years
4 years
5 years

You can tell how old some molluscs are by counting the growth-rings on their shells.

You may see crabs on the beach and amongst rocks too. Hermit Crabs live in the empty shells of other animals.

DROWNED CRAB FACT

Not all crabs live in the sea. The Robber Crab will drown if it stays in water too long!

Robber Crab

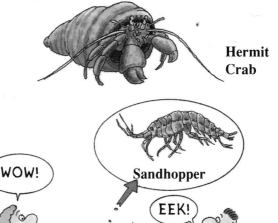

Hermit Crab

Sandhopper

WOW!

EEK!

PING!

PONG!

ZIPP!

You'll see plenty of seaweed on the shore too. Seaweed provides homes for lots of different types of animals. Gently lift a clump and look underneath. But be careful. Lots of little things like this will jump out!..

BEACHCOMBING

BUT... not just plants and animals are washed up on the beach.
People have been dropping things in the sea for thousands of years...

Treasure from old wrecks

Old coins

I have been lost on a desert island for 26 years. I am worried I may have left the oven switched on. I'm sure my sausages will be burned by now. Please go to my house and find out. There is a map on the other side. X marks the spot!

Bottles with messages inside

Some people make a living from searching for washed-up items on beaches. This is called beachcombing...

... but they don't do it like this!

HOW TO BEACHCOMB

HAH!

1. Always watch where you're walking.

2. Look out for clumps of washed-up items. These are called flotsam.

3. Items of the same size and weight are often washed up in the same place. Look out for patches of small pebbles. You may be lucky and find modern coins or jewelry.

FINDING METAL

But... be careful. During the Second World War, millions of bombs and mines were dropped into the sea. Some of them didn't explode! They may be washed up on your beach. If you find something which may be dangerous...

1. Don't touch it.

2. Mark the spot.

3. Telephone the police.

You might try searching for coins with a metal detector. But be careful how you use it...

BLEEP! BLEEP!

WHOOPS!

1. Don't forget to fill in any holes you make!

PING! PING! PING!

PONK!

2. Don't disturb other people who want to use the beach.

3. You'll find a lot of cans, ring-pulls and bottle tops. Don't just throw this rubbish back onto the beach!

Put it into a litter bin. Or take it home for recycling!

LITTER BIN

DUNES AND DUMPERS

You'll find lots of litter on crowded beaches and in sand dunes. Picnic rubbish spoils everybody's fun. So... don't be a dune dumper!..

BOTTLES

Take your bottles home with you.

Seagulls have very good eyesight!

– squawk! – What do you fancy today Ethel?

– waak! – The quiche looks good!

I fancy that toe!

I'm sure I had FIVE toes on that foot this morning!

RUBBISH

Leftover food and food containers attract flies and stinging insects. Wasp stings and sandfly bites are very painful. Put your leftover food in a litter bin. Or feed the seagulls with it!..

CANS

Sharp-edged metal cans are a menace too. Take your cans home with you.

Well you shouldn't have bought so many in the first place!

You've dropped one!

GASP!

CAN COLLECTING FACT

Some metal detecting clubs get together each year for can-finding contests. The winner gets a prize from the local council. This helps to keep beaches free of cans.

CLAP! CLAP!

~ GOLDEN CAN AWARD ~

ALL WASHED UP!

You may find other sorts of rubbish on beaches too...

CONTAINERS

Ships often carry freight containers on their decks. About three hundred of them are lost overboard every year. One may end up on your beach. Never try to open a container. There may be something dangerous inside!

LUMPS OF OIL

Sometimes you'll see lumps of crude oil like this. Oil often leaks from oil tankers and other ships. It can stick to birds' feathers and stop them from flying.

If you find an oily bird on your beach, call for the local animal rescue society.

Oil can also stick to you!

HOW TO CLEAN OFF OIL

You can use some types of sun-tan cream to loosen oil on your skin. Mix it with some fine sand and rub it on gently. Then wash it off in the sea.

DUMPING TOWNS

Some towns on the coast use the ocean as a rubbish dump. Millions of tonnes of household waste are dropped into the sea every year. About half of it is paper, cardboard and waste food.
This is called organic waste.

There are billions of tiny life-forms called plankton in the sea. Plankton can eat organic waste.

But... plankton can't eat the other half of the rubbish. This includes plastic, rubber, metals and household chemicals. So this rubbish is often washed back onto the beach.

Dolphins, seals and sea birds may get caught up in rubbish such as plastic bags.

SEWAGE

Human waste products are called sewage. Sometimes raw sewage is pumped straight into the sea.
You can catch diseases from sewage.
So... it's best not to play near sewage drains like this...

DUMPING SHIPS

Ships pollute the sea too. Oil tankers carry up to two hundred thousand tonnes of crude oil at a time!
When they're not carrying oil, sea water is pumped into the empty tanks. This stops the ship from rolling about too much.

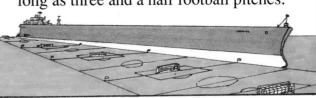

This sea water mixes with the leftover oil. Later, the tanks are emptied to make room for more oil. So the leftover oil is pumped into the sea too.
Tankers pump about one million tonnes of oil into the sea each year.

eek!

Many other poisonous wastes are dumped into the sea. Drums of chemicals may wash up on your beach. Some are marked with symbols which tell you that the contents are dangerous. BUT... some drums don't have any warning sign at all!

SPOT THE DANGEROUS DRUM!

Which of these washed-up drums are safe to go near?

ANSWER: Only drum **F**, because... **A** = The contents will burn you. **B** = Deadly poison. **C** = More deadly poison! **D** = Radioactive waste. **E** = You don't know what's inside!

THE FOOD CHAIN

All the living things in the sea depend on each other for food.
Big fish eat small fish. Small fish eat tiny fish, and so on. This is called a food chain. Here's an example...

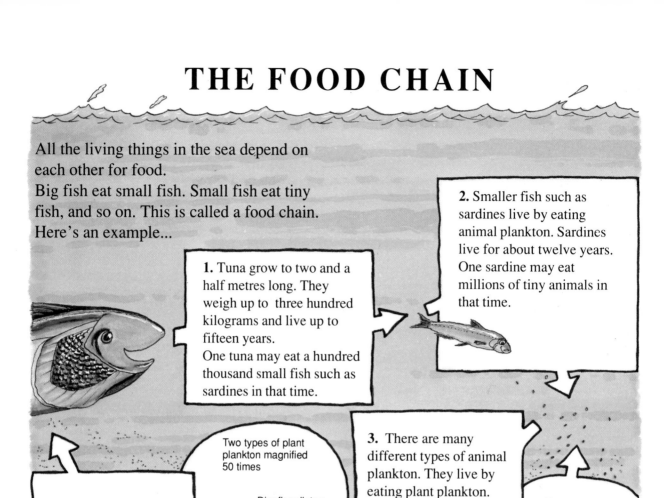

2. Smaller fish such as sardines live by eating animal plankton. Sardines live for about twelve years. One sardine may eat millions of tiny animals in that time.

1. Tuna grow to two and a half metres long. They weigh up to three hundred kilograms and live up to fifteen years.
One tuna may eat a hundred thousand small fish such as sardines in that time.

Two types of plant plankton magnified 50 times

Dinoflagellates

Diatoms

3. There are many different types of animal plankton. They live by eating plant plankton. One tiny animal may eat thousands of plants in its lifetime.

Two types of plankton magnified 15 times

Copepod

Pteropod

4. There are billions of tiny plants in the sea. The droppings from fish provide food for the tiny plants!

People come into this food chain too. You may have eaten tuna or sardines recently. BUT... we have to be careful not to break the food chain. What happens if we catch too many sardines for example?
The tuna will have less to eat and may starve to death. And... more animal plankton will survive and eat more plants. Then there'll be fewer plants!

Humph!.. No sardines to eat! I'm starving!

Tuna

Animal plankton

Goody goody! No sardines to eat us!

AND... we have to be careful not to poison the food chain too!

Almost all of the Earth's water is in the sea. People who dump chemical wastes in it say that a few extra tonnes of poisons won't make any difference.

BUT... they're wrong!

FOOD CHAIN POISON PUZZLE!

Take another look at the food chain on page 12. Imagine...

1. If each plant plankton eats a particle of poison from a leaking drum of waste...

2. If each animal plankton eats a thousand plant plankton...

3. If each sardine eats a million tiny animals...

4. If each tuna eats a hundred thousand sardines...

How many particles of chemical waste will there be inside the tuna?

Answer: 100,000,000,000,000,000

Deadly poisons such as lead and mercury may collect inside plants and animals in the sea.
When the larger animals eat them they take in the poison too!

MINAMATA MERCURY FACT

In the 1950's a factory in Japan dumped mercury waste in the sea. It got into the local food chain and poisoned people in a fishing port called Minamata. Mercury damages the brain and the nerves.

BUT... accidents like this don't happen very often. So don't worry too much— fresh fish are still safe to eat!

FISH FACTS

Fishing boats catch about eighty million tonnes of fish each year.

There are about twenty thousand different sorts of fish. But we only use about thirty different types for food.

This fishing ship is called a stern trawler.

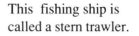

Shoal of sardines

Some fish, such as tuna, are big enough to catch with a fishing rod. But most of the fish we eat are caught with nets.

Some types of fish swim in groups called shoals. So a big net can catch thousands of fish at once. Some types of fish are in danger of dying out because we catch too many of them.

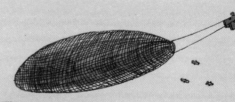

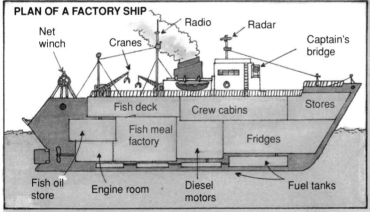

PLAN OF A FACTORY SHIP

Net winch — Radio — Radar — Captain's bridge — Cranes — Fish deck — Crew cabins — Stores — Fish meal factory — Fridges — Fish oil store — Engine room — Diesel motors — Fuel tanks

Large modern fishing boats are called factory ships. They turn the fish into fish meal, fish fillets and fish fingers. Fish meal is made into food for farm animals. Overfishing by factory ships can badly affect local fishing industries.

DANGEROUS DRIFT-NET FACT

Some fishing ships use large drift-nets. They catch any fish that happen along. But... they often trap whales, dolphins and seals too! These animals can easily drown in a drift-net because they breathe air.

OCEAN EXPERT FISHING CODE

1. Only catch fish to eat, not for fun.
2. Put young, small fish back in the water so that they get a chance to grow.
3. Try eating different types of fish for a change.

WHALES AND SHARKS

WHALES

Whales, dolphins and seals aren't fish. They're mammals. A mammal is an animal which produces milk for its young. The Blue Whale can weigh up to 160 tonnes and is the largest animal in the world. A baby Blue Whale needs about half a tonne of milk a day! Until recently, whaling ships caught so many whales that some types almost died out. Nowadays, most whales are protected by international law.

SHARKS

There are three hundred and eighty different types of shark. Some types will eat you if they catch you! Here are three dangerous ones...

HUMPBACK WHALE FACT

Some whales are able to find food by making loud noises. They listen to the echoes which bounce back to them. They can recognise objects this way. Humpback whales also sing to each other over long distances to find a mate.

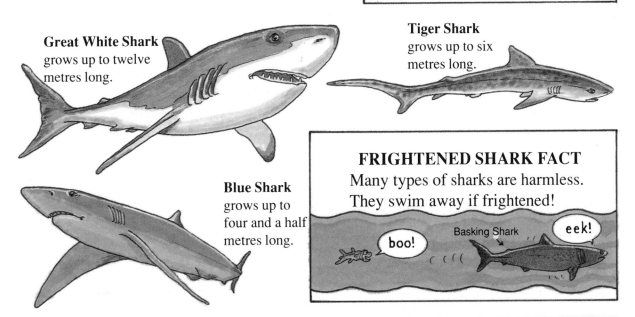

Great White Shark grows up to twelve metres long.

Tiger Shark grows up to six metres long.

Blue Shark grows up to four and a half metres long.

FRIGHTENED SHARK FACT
Many types of sharks are harmless. They swim away if frightened!

Basking Shark

boo!

eek!

SHARK STEAK FACT
More sharks are eaten by people than people are eaten by sharks!

SEA FOOD

As well as fish, we can eat all sorts of other sea food too!

SEAWEED

Seaweed contains valuable food chemicals such as iodine. Some types are grown on seaweed farms in Japan.

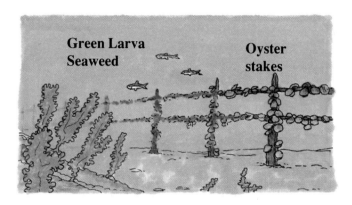

Sometimes valuable pearls form inside oysters!..

SHELLFISH

Shellfish such as oysters and mussels are also grown for food. Oyster farmers put wooden stakes into the sea bed. The oysters attach themselves to the stakes. The shellfish are collected when they're big enough to eat.

LOBSTERS

We also eat larger animals such as crabs and lobsters. Lobster catchers use lobster pots to trap them. They work like this...

KRILL CATCH FEAR FACT

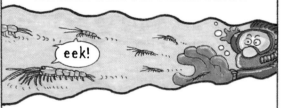

Krill are distant relatives of lobsters. They look like tiny shrimps, and are food for some whales and fish. Fishing vessels catch about 500,000 tonnes of krill each year. Some sea experts are worried that we are catching too many krill.

The more krill people eat, the less there are for the other sea animals to live on.

1. The lobster sees or smells the dead fish bait in the lobster pot.

2. It climbs in the trapdoor on the top to eat the bait.

3. The door springs shut and the lobster can't get out!

Female salmon

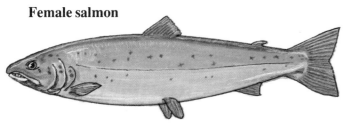

Male sea trout

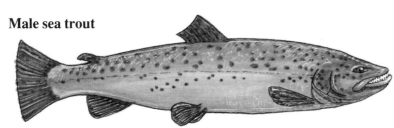

FARM FISH

Some types of fish such as trout and salmon are grown in large pools on fish farms. It's easier to catch them if they're in an artificial pool. They're fed with special food so that they grow quickly.

The type of food they eat also affects what they taste like.

Some fish farmers try to improve the taste of fish by adding chemical flavours to fish food!!

BE AN EXPERT FISH EATER!..

Fresh sea food is usually very good for your health. But some fish are poisonous. And some parts of fish are poisonous too. If you catch your own fish to eat...

1. Don't eat anything unless you know what it is.

2. Make sure all the insides are cut out before you cook it.

3. Watch out for bones!

FUN AT SEA

Large ships and boats are used for fishing and transport. These days, most small boats are used for pleasure...

Fishing

GOT ONE!

Silly humans!

Quiet sunbathing

Water-skiing

WAP!

Racing

BUT... motor boats are bad for wildlife. The outboard motors can injure and kill slow-moving animals and fish. Manatees are mammals which eat plants in shallow water. They are often found with propeller scars on their backs.

SAILING

Sailing boats are more healthy and can be better fun than motor boats. They are powered by the wind instead of smoky motors.

TOOT! TOOT!

WINDSURFING

Windsurfing is great fun too. But you need to be an expert to do it properly. Watch people windsurfing. You'll notice that they spend a lot of time falling in the water!

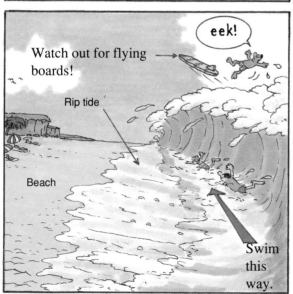

Watch out for flying boards!

Rip tide

Beach

Swim this way.

SURF FUN TIPS

Surfing is a lot harder than it looks!

At first find a beach with small waves and no rocks. A big wave can hit you with the force of a truckload of bricks!

If you lose your board, relax and let the waves carry you to the beach. Don't try to swim against the rip tide. This is the wave water running back into the sea. Get to the beach by swimming alongside it. Take deep breaths when you can, and let the waves get you to the shore.
Have fun!

Of course for all these activities you need to be able to swim!..

IN THE SWIM

Swimming is the best exercise for staying fit and healthy.

You can get swimming lessons at most leisure centres and schools.

Swimming pools are easier to swim in than the sea. Practice diving and underwater swimming until you're good at it.

Once you've learned how to swim properly, take a dip in the sea. It's great fun sharing the water with other animals!

Swimming in the sea is quite safe if you watch what you're doing...

SAFE SEA SWIMMING

1. Watch for a red flag like this. It means it's not safe to swim.

2. And don't dive in without looking. You never know what's just beneath the surface!

IN THE DEEP

Fish breathe tiny bubbles of oxygen in the water. They can't breathe air because it's not damp enough. And water's too damp for people to breathe!

BUT... you can use a snorkel to swim just under the surface. This helps you to breathe with your head beneath the water.

Some people join a sub-aqua club and learn how to swim underwater.

HOW TO TUBE-WATCH

If you can't swim, you can still watch the sea wildlife. It's hard to see through the surface ripples. So try this...

1. Get an old plastic bucket.
2. Cut out the bottom
3. Use it like this...

ooo!

SNIFF!

BARRACUDA

Divers breathe from the tanks of compressed air which they carry on their backs.

Sea water can be very cold a few metres down, so divers wear a rubber wet suit to help keep them warm. It also protects them from sharp rocks. A bleeding wound may attract dangerous fish such as sharks and barracuda.

Barracuda hunt in packs for fish. They see people as just another odd type of fish!

Fish float because they have a sac of air in their bodies.

DO YOU FLOAT?..

Your body is just light enough to float in water too. That's partly because you contain trapped air. Air is lighter than water, so it helps you to float. You can see this working in the bath...

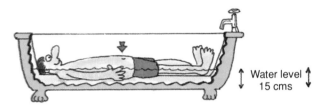

↕ Water level ↕ 15 cms

1. Keep your head above the water! Relax your body and breathe right out. You'll sink a bit.

2. Keep your head above the water! Then breathe in, so your lungs are full of air. You'll find your body floats higher in the water.

You can float better in the sea. The sea has lots of salt in it, so it's heavier than tap water.

1. Float a heavy piece of wood in a bowl of tap water.	**2.** Pour in some table salt and stir it round.	**3.** Now the wood floats higher in the water!

WHY THE SEA IS SALTY FACT

Sea water and rocks contain thousands of different chemicals. These are washed from the land to the sea by rivers. The most common of these chemicals is called sodium chloride. This is better known as table salt!

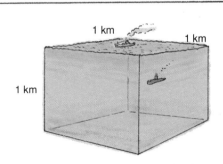

1 km

1 km

1 km

A cube of sea water this size contains 40 tonnes of salt!

A PINCH OF SALT...

Most seafish can't live in fresh water. They need the salt which passes through their bodies. The sodium in salt helps their nerves to carry messages. All animals have nerves, and they all need salt to stay alive.

SEAFISH FLESH FACT

Sea fish don't contain much salt. Their bodies don't need to store it because they live in salty water.

A litre of blood contains about the same amount of salt as a litre of sea water.

In some parts of the world, people collect salt from the sea...

BUT fresh water fish and land animals don't live in salty water. So they have to carry their own supply of salt with them. Next time you cut yourself, taste your blood. It's a bit salty!..

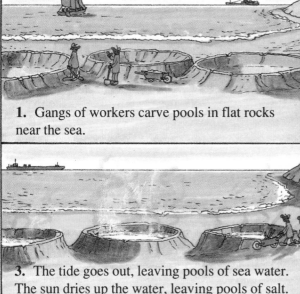

1. Gangs of workers carve pools in flat rocks near the sea.

3. The tide goes out, leaving pools of sea water. The sun dries up the water, leaving pools of salt.

2. The tide fills up the pools with sea water.

4. People come and collect the salt before the next tide comes in.

TIME AND TIDE

All objects in the Universe attract each other with a force called gravity.
You are being attracted by the Earth when you fall out of a tree!..

The Earth attracts the Moon and the Moon attracts the Earth. But don't worry – the Moon won't fall on the Earth!

The Moon travels round the Earth once every twenty-eight days. It's travelling just fast enough to stop it falling on the Earth. And... it's travelling just slow enough to stop it from flying off into space!

The sea bulges out a bit here. (High tide)

[NOT TO SCALE]

Earth → Moon's gravity → Moon

The sea becomes more shallow here. (Low tide)

About three quarters of the Earth's surface is water. The Moon's gravity is strong enough to slightly attract this water and make it bulge. The Earth spins once every twenty four hours. The bulge is always directly underneath the moon. This is what causes high and low tides. But that's not all!...

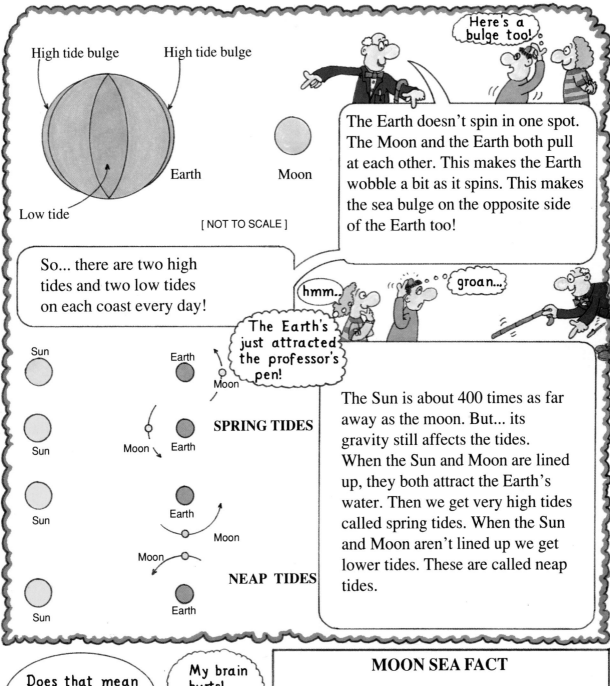

High tide bulge   High tide bulge

Earth   Moon

Low tide

[NOT TO SCALE]

Here's a bulge too!

The Earth doesn't spin in one spot. The Moon and the Earth both pull at each other. This makes the Earth wobble a bit as it spins. This makes the sea bulge on the opposite side of the Earth too!

So... there are two high tides and two low tides on each coast every day!

The Earth's just attracted the professor's pen!

hmm..   groan...

Sun   Earth   Moon

SPRING TIDES

Sun   Moon   Earth

Sun   Earth   Moon

Sun   Moon   Earth

NEAP TIDES

Sun   Earth

The Sun is about 400 times as far away as the moon. But... its gravity still affects the tides. When the Sun and Moon are lined up, they both attract the Earth's water. Then we get very high tides called spring tides. When the Sun and Moon aren't lined up we get lower tides. These are called neap tides.

Does that mean that the Moon has tides too?

My brain hurts!

NOG! NOG!

Good question. But...

MOON SEA FACT

People used to think that there were seas on the moon. They invented sea names for flat plains which they thought were water. Now that people have been there, we know that there's no open water on the moon.

ICE AND WATER

The Sun does more than help to make tides. It also heats up the sea, making the water move in currents. These currents can move floating objects for thousands of kilometers.

It's too cold to swim today!

North Pole

South pole

Some parts of the world don't get much sunshine. So at the North and South poles for example, water freezes.
A thick layer of ice and snow called an ice cap forms. Large chunks break off and float away on the currents. These chunks are called icebergs.

There are billions of litres of frozen water in the ice caps.
If it all melted, the sea level would rise. Some scientists think that coastlines would be flooded with fifty metres of water. And many of the world's big cities are near the coast!..

New York might look like this if the ice caps melted!

LONDON!   SYDNEY!   AMSTERDAM!!

This could happen because weather experts say that the Earth is getting warmer! This is because of the...

GREENHOUSE EFFECT!..

Have you got a greenhouse in your garden?

A greenhouse becomes very hot because the glass traps the Sun's heat.

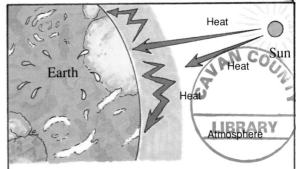

The Earth's atmosphere acts like the glass of a greenhouse. Gases called carbon dioxide and methane trap the Sun's heat.

More and more carbon dioxide and methane is being pumped into the air every day...

From burning forests...

From car exhausts.
(transport)

From factories and power stations.
(energy)

...and cattle and sheep!
(farming)

So more and more heat is trapped in the atmosphere!

HELPING THE ICE-CAPS...

You can help to slow down the Greenhouse Effect...

1. Get your parents and friends to use their cars less.

2. Use less energy. Remember to switch off lights and heaters.

3. Plants take in carbon dioxide and produce oxygen.
   So... plant some trees!

THE WATER CYCLE

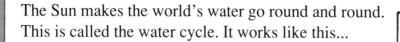

The Sun makes the world's water go round and round. This is called the water cycle. It works like this...

1. The sun heats up the sea. Steam rises to form clouds.

2. The wind blows the clouds towards the land.

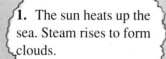

3. The clouds reach cool air. Sometimes this is over the sea, sometimes over the land. The clouds become heavy with water. Rain falls. Rivers take the rainwater back to the sea.

Nice cup of tea

Steam

Ice

Metal tray

Boil some water near a bowl of ice.

The steam cools and turns to water on the cold bowl. Water collects in the tray.

You can see a water cycle happening in your own home. Get an adult to help you with this experiment...

You can empty the tray of water back into the kettle. Then start again!

Streams and rivers join together to form a large river near the coast. This wide tidal part is called an estuary.
All sorts of plants and wildlife live in estuaries.

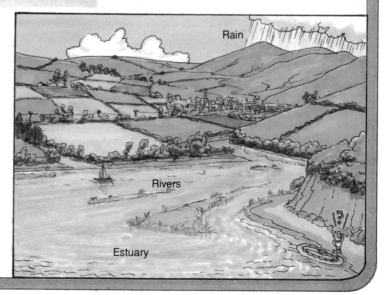

Rain

Rivers

Estuary

ESTUARIES

BUT... people like to use estuaries too! They build boat marinas, campsites, hotels, leisure centres and so on. The pollution from these activities can ruin estuaries. Poisonous chemicals which farmers use can drain into estuaries. And rivers bring pollution from towns upstream too!..

BE A WILDLIFE SAVER!

Some of the world's estuaries have been made into Nature Reserves to protect wildlife.

But... other places need looking after too. You can help. Start a wildlife protection club at your school. Then you can help to look after local wildlife when you come back from the beach!

BE AN ESTUARY SAVER!..

1. Never throw rubbish into estuaries or rivers.

2. Don't disturb wildlife, especially birds and their eggs. Lots of people used to collect birds eggs. Some types of birds have died out because of egg collecting. Some eggs are protected by law!..

Wildlife protection club in action!

People like to take home **SOUVENIRS** of their holidays...

Malachite

Agate

Opal

Fluorite

These stones have been cut with a special saw, then polished.

Why not start a rock collection? You'll find lots of beautiful pebbles on most beaches. Some ordinary-looking stones have amazing patterns inside. Break a few open with a sharp hammer and see.

Collect some shells too.

Then you can make models of animals and other things with them!..

You can buy stones and shells from beach souvenir shops.
Conch and sea-urchin shells look very pretty. But... they aren't often washed up on the beach in one piece. So people dive and collect these shells from the sea-bed. Then the animals inside are boiled alive to kill them, leaving the shells.

THE BARRIER REEF STORY

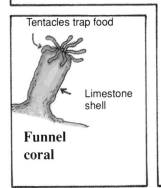

Tentacles trap food

Limestone shell

Funnel coral

Tiny animals called corals also have shells. They are made of limestone too. Each type clumps together in different ways to form odd growths. They look a bit like stone plants!..

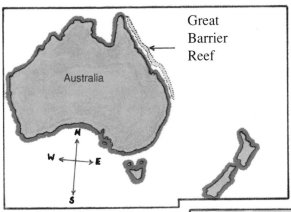

Great Barrier Reef

Australia

N W E S

As old corals die, new ones grow on top of them. After thousands of years, huge piles of corals called coral reefs form. The largest one is the Great Barrier Reef near Australia. This is a home for thousands of types of sea life.
BUT... look what happens when tourists interfere with the reef...

A spiky starfish called the Crown of Thorns eat corals.

MUNCH! MUNCH!

Shellfish called tritons eat these starfish.

eek! LEAP!

But... divers collect tritons to sell to tourists.

So with fewer tritons around, the starfish can eat more corals...

MUNCHY MUNCH!

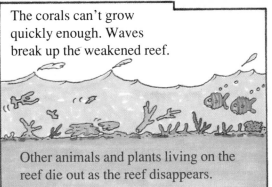

The corals can't grow quickly enough. Waves break up the weakened reef.

Other animals and plants living on the reef die out as the reef disappears.

So... tourists taking just a few souvenirs home can damage other wildlife too!
You can pick up souvenirs from the beach...
But make sure they're dead first!

NIP!!

nnn!

Now that you've read this book, you'll know a bit about what goes on in the sea. But you're not an ocean expert yet!
Keep your eyes open next time you visit the coast.
You may be in for a

surprise!

Every living thing on our planet depends on the sea. It's up to us to look after it.
The more you know about the sea, the more you'll be able to help its wildlife. So...

GET WET SOON!

INDEX